The Thread Box

A COLLECTION OF POEMS

by

June Hall McCash

Copyright © 2014 June Hall McCash
All rights reserved
This book may not be reproduced or transmitted, in whole or in part, through any means electronic or mechanical including photocopying or electronic transmission without prior written permission from the author, except short excerpts considered normal for review.

ISBN-13: 978-1-937937-05-8

First Edition

Printed in The United States of America

Twin Oaks Press
twinoakspress@gmail.com
www.twinoakspress.com

Design
Art Growden

Cover Illustration
Susanne Hebden

Begin to weave, and God will provide the thread.
Old German Proverb

TABLE OF CONTENTS

I. THE JEKYLL POEMS

To the Islands in December 3
Reconciliation 4
North End Beach... 5
Our Last Winter at Jekyll... 6
North End Beach II 7
Late Winter Day on Jekyll Island............................... 8
Beach Walk 9
Photo From Crane Cottage 10
Pulitzer's Offering 11
Paper Fish 12
Morning Ride... 13
Wildflowers on the Causeway................................... 14
Jekyll Map 15

II. POEMS OF CHILDHOOD AND FAMILY

Radio Lessons 19
War Letters 21
Sunday Rides 22
The Mourner... 24
Prologue 25
Aubade for My Mother 26
To My Lost Grandfather 27
Grandmother at Prayer 29
Papa Gailey 31
Return to Buckhead 32

III. POEMS OF THE ARTS

On Coming Upon the Grave of Andrew Lytle
at the Sewanee Writers Conference 37
Starry Night... 39
The Craft and Sullen Art... 40
Water Dreams.. 41
Poem.. 42
Solitary Harpist at the Sewanee Music Festival ... 44
Concours Poétique 45

IV. ANIMAL AND NATURE POEMS

Layover in Cincinnati 49
Return from Russia 50
Entr'acte 51
Sunday Morning in Key West 52
Metamorphosis 53
Spring Day in Seattle 54
Revisit 55
Winter Fragment 56
Spring Fragment 57
Day of the Empress 58
Eclipse on Mount Washington on a Cloudy Night ... 59
Uncle Ed's Hound Dog 60
Summer Days Have No Bones 61
Subdivision Rising 62

V. POEMS OF LOVE AND LOSS

Valentine 65
Photo for a Second Marriage 66
Contraceptive 67
Viriditas 68
Without Goodbye 69
The Garden 71
Haiku 72
Anniversary, February 8, 2011 73
The Gift 74
Love 75
Billets Doux 76
Weekend on the Mountain 77
First Love 78
Love After Prime 79

VI. POEMS FOR THE MEDIEVAL SOUL

Tapestry 83
Sonnet à mon bel ami 84
Heloise and Abelard Sequence
   I. Heloise To Abelard 85
   II. Tomb of Heloise and Abelard 86

    III. Père Lachaise 88
Laüstic 89
Eleanor 90
Burgundian Mirror, Fifteenth Century 91
The Postulate 92
Chevrefoil 93
Lyric 94
The Thread Box... 95

ACKNOWLEDGMENTS.. 97

I dedicate this volume to all those I love and to the memories of those I have loved and lost.

I. THE JEKYLL ISLAND POEMS

TO THE ISLAND IN DECEMBER

We drive in sullen silence
through the unexpected storm.
Cold wet pellets strike the windshield
penetrating a determined fog.
No wild verbena lines the way,
purpling grasses by the roadside's edge
like we saw in summer months.
Now only flashes of gray stalks
catch in the headlights,
our disgruntled hush
muted by the motor's roar
and thumps of raindrops
pelting glass.

We watch the road that stretches
toward the sea, toward memories
of sunlit shallows on the shore
and clumps of golden foam
scudding across the sand,
luring us on with secret hope,
almost like certainty.
I only pray this storm will pass,
and an equally determined sun
will pierce our troubled dark
and pour on us like grace
relentless streams
of welcome winter light.

RECONCILIATION

The smell of damp earth fills late afternoon
as a distant cannonade of thunder rolls
across the island. The sky grows dark
and heavy. No rain yet, but rain will come —
it's in the air, threatening and thick.
Pine trees bend as clouds grow blacker still.
A slash of lightning splits the sky.
Wind whips my hair, driving me inside
to await the wild percussion of the rain.
It does not come. The wind dies down,
Thunder calms. The storm drifts out to sea.
At twilight, when I least expect,
a warm and gentle rain begins to fall,
pattering like forgiveness on the roof.

NORTH END BEACH

Tilting seaward,
black roots exposed
by winter tides,
the oak still stood
upright last year,
oblivious
to the blades of rain
and northeast winds
snatching at its branches.
Two hundred years
it stood, as taller trunks
were cut for masts and timber
and weaker trees
were torn away
by autumn storms
or split by lightning's slash.
It was a certain landmark
in this island world
where all is flux.

Yet now brought down
by wind and tide,
its stark new beauty
parable in this
place of peace,
where even the fallen
can be redeemed.

OUR LAST WINTER AT JEKYLL

Tomorrow we must leave,
as always,
but today we are here,
together,
to watch
the terns and gulls
and winter scaups,
bobbing like dark corks
on the choppy sea.
Foam sweeps the beach
as northeast winds
toss the pines
and sea grasses.
A solitary figure,
dark against a dull gray sky,
walks the empty beach.
I see myself next year,
alone,
bent forward
against an icy wind.

NORTH END BEACH II

Broken shells and bracken
wash up in the May tide
on this island drifting south,
natural detritus
among the dark
bones of fallen trees
sculpted
by wind and sea.

I should like
to leave behind
such stark remains,
in wildly crafted words
that tell the tale
of life too soon
and slowly
swept away.

LATE WINTER DAY ON JEKYLL ISLAND

From leaden clouds
rain falls in slow, sparse drops.
Light scarcely penetrates
the scrim settled
over the dripping woods.
I expect no interruptions here,
for who would venture out
on such a day?

No bird songs pierce the calm.
No squirrels scurry across the yard,
pausing, posing gray statues
against the damp, brown grass.
The osprey's nest, drenched,
abandoned, still perches
on a black branch
against the metal sky.

Camellias bud, a hint of crimson petticoat,
just visible beneath late winter's lifted skirt.

BEACH WALK

From last night's storm the sand
is strewn with empty shells,
some broken beyond recognition,
their jagged edges testimonial
to dramas of the ocean floor.
The beach is empty
except for screaming gulls
and pelicans swooping for breakfast
over the cresting wave.
The starless world is gray
before the bright yolk of sun
breaks and spills across the sea.

In my now solitary walk
I thread my way among
the fractured shells,
trying not to cut my feet
and leave my blood upon
this pre-dawn shore.
The broken whelk is cool
and damp against my cheek.
It smells of the salty creature
that lay inside and once found comfort there.
There is solace in the hardness of that shell,
the wrecked beauty of its remains.

From the translucent rose of its inner room,
a cameo could still be carved.

PHOTO FROM CRANE COTTAGE

The morning sun fades
from the balcony's pot
of red geraniums.
Palm trees point
toward the darkling sky,
echoed by the steeple
of Faith Chapel—all framed
by the room's French doors—
the perfect photo captured
on the emulsion of my mind.

I step outside.
The rising wind,
smelling of damp earth,
whips against my face.

A couple, hand-in-hand, strolls
on the crushed-shell road below,
unaware of my presence,
ignoring the storm clouds
gathering overhead.

A gargoyle guards
the Tiffany window
of the chapel's facade
and waits, head down,
to regurgitate the coming rain.

PULITZER'S OFFERING*

He brought me violets
this morning
from his ride
through the dew
along the bridle path —
violets he'd stopped
to gather beneath
dripping branches
of live oaks
and unfurling fronds
of resurrection ferns.

The tiny bouquet
speaks not so much
affection for me
as longing
for his absent wife.
I am but surrogate,
my hands a vase
to receive those wildflowers
I always knew were hers.

---

*Joseph Pulitzer, in the absence of his wife Kate at Jekyll Island in 1904, sometimes invited Jean Struthers, the daughter of his next-door neighbor in Moss Cottage, to join him in his morning horseback rides. Once, when he rode without her, he brought her a small bouquet of violets.

PAPER FISH

Her back to wind and dunes, facing
ocean swells, she sets her heels
to reel it in. It fights, darts,
soars, swimming ocean air,
tail flapping at the breeze,
defiant, struggling to be free.

She gives it line but keeps it taut,
holds steady, tension pulling tight,
then starts to wind the line again
around the spool to reel it down.
It leaps, ducks, and swerves once more,
bright colors flashing in the sun.

Now she reaches out her hand
and closes fingers like a net
to seize its struts and try to calm
its restless body, almost lifeless,
except for the length of tail
still whipping in the eager wind.

MORNING RIDE

I love to watch the morning sun
crawl down the tallest pines,
overwhelm the shadow
of the house, and claim the day.
When it reaches the bottom
of the trees, the time has come
to don my helmet and set sail
on my bike through early light.

The trail I choose varies,
sometimes beside the sea,
through sunlit marshes
or along the woodland route.
Brown-nosed deer, lizards,
sand crabs, even small alligators
scamper to clear my path
and scurry to the roadway's edge.

All but butterflies.
Oblivious to my coming,
their flutterings unpredictable,
they never veer aside
as my body hurtles toward them.
They drift like slow sunlight,
as I dodge this way or that
to keep from crushing fragile wings
and give them one more day of life.

WILDFLOWERS ON THE CAUSEWAY

We leave the island, leave the sea behind
to head once more toward the interstate.
Beside the causeway, grassy slopes, lined
with wildflowers in profusion, replicate
plein air paintings. Impressionists could imitate
such beauty born of light. Like them, I long
to capture God's reds and golds and emulate
their mastery. In arrogance I assign myself
to paint those many hues in verse,
to speak those shades so hard to recreate.

But words prove insufficient to portray
wild blooms that take my lexicon away.

JEKYLL MAP

The creek snakes
between the marshes
and the island's leeward side,
widening at the point
where the old club stands today.

The island is the soft shape
of an aqua velvet slipper,
trimmed in pale rose embroidery,
pointed at the toe, carelessly
abandoned beneath a canopy
of live oaks and Spanish moss.

The marshy leg,
veined by a silk-stocking
seam of causeway now,
runs westward
toward the mainland.

It adorns my study wall
and takes me there,
where warmer breezes blow
and soft-eyed deer lie down
among palmetto fronds,
and where a gentler pace
urges on my pen.

II. POEMS OF CHILDHOOD AND FAMILY

RADIO LESSONS

When I came home from school,
my grandmother was ironing,
listening to *Stella Dallas*
and *Backstage Wife*
on the radio.
I entertained myself
with paper dolls
and jacks
until her programs ended
and mine began.

At five o'clock
she put her apron on
and went to the kitchen
to make the dough,
cut the biscuits,
and put on green beans
for supper.
For half an hour
I had adventures
with the Lone Ranger
and Tonto.

And thus, we waited
on wartime afternoons,
my grandmother and I,
for Mama to come home.

Those slow days
shaped me,
as I learned
to wait my turn,
play by myself,

see with my mind,
eat my Cheerios,
and unravel the secrets
of decoder rings.

WAR LETTERS

Browning, brittle pages, one written on toilet tissue
for paper was scarce, his letters fill three boxes,
one almost every day while he was gone,
each carefully preserved in its envelope by my mother.

The letters tell of trivia—weather, bombed-out sites,
patterns of frost on an occasional window pane—
except for rare moments, when anxieties pierce the page.
He wrote no letters during that long week
in Bastogne, though letters came later from the hospital,
revealing, not the danger, but his inability to write.
Times had been hard in that hole he'd dug in the earth.
Only later did we learn of fear and frostbite
and the shell that landed in his abandoned foxhole,
after something told him to dig another farther on,
and he'd obeyed.
He thought he'd heard God's voice
in those white woods that night,
as the mindless shells rained down
from all directions. He covered his head and recited
the Twenty-third Psalm, the only one he knew by heart.
It was enough.

SUNDAY RIDES

Our family used to take long rides
on summer Sunday afternoons,
car windows open to the breeze,
far into the countryside.

Daddy would sometimes make a stop
to buy us ice cream cones
and breathe the country air,
while Mama picked a crop

of daisies from the roadway's edge.
It was that part of Sunday
I liked best—bee-buzzing silence,
sweet smell of flowering hedge,

a greening stretch of planted fields,
the scent of fresh-plowed earth,
wildflowers blooming all around,
sunlight glinting off the wheels.

When we came to a standstill
I would go to the front of the car
to pick dead butterflies
from off the radiator grill

and with tiny fingers trace
the delicate designs of inert wings,
pondering their fragility
pondering their grace.

The unfathomable purpose
of their meandering
led them nowhere but to death.
I wondered at the pathos

of their pace so lackadaisical
that caught them in the grillwork
amazingly undestroyed, yet
with an impact so brutal

their bodies were compressed.
Yet their wings remained intact
like dusty, billowed sails
not yet come to rest.

I recall those Sunday outings
with a certain fondness now
that butterflies are rarer,
a memory of simpler things,

of a world that seemed still new,
with greening fields so strewn
with wildflowers and butterflies
the world could even spare a few.

THE MOURNER

He stood among the shadow faces
by my father's grave.
No one saw him standing there,
for he had come from far away
and out of distant years.
When he bent to sorrow
with my mother, she couldn't
see him either through her tears.

He said his name. She looked up.
In tender shock of recognition,
she reached for his outstretched hand.
Together those wrinkled hands embraced
a young, translucent time before
that centered on that figure gone,
when they had loved each other
but they loved my father more.

PROLOGUE

When she was turning ninety-four,
my mother took me down to see
her grandmother's house,
the house where she was born.
Rotting on its joists, the floors were caving in,
though, she pointed out with pride,
the tin roof still held off the rain.

She painted for me her childhood there,
spring orchard blooms, fall fruits laid out to dry
on the rooftop of the barn for winter's store,
the henhouse where once a fox got in,
the old well, now sealed, but where
the water drawn was sweet and pure and cool.

The pride and love she felt for that old house
and those who used to live inside, told on her face
and in her voice — all that before my tale began.

Three Octobers later
we buried her in the graveyard
beside the old granite church —
where her husband and baby girl,
parents and grandparents lie.
The service ended, I took my sons
and their sons to see the house,
prologue to their lives as well.
Dressed in funeral clothes
and holding hands, together
we watched the little dark-haired girl
playing in the orchard, the one
they knew so well as Grandma,
without whom we would not have been.

AUBADE FOR MY MOTHER

One morning she awoke
and refused to open her eyes
again to admit
the so-called verity of dawn,
the brumous vision,
plaintive voices
rising from other rooms,
and antiseptic failure to mask
endless maculations.

Rather she lay content
with clear visions of sliced apples
lying like neat windrows
drying on the barn's tin roof,
the warm smoothness of the nested egg,
off which she'd just shooed
the clucking hen,
the wafting smell of biscuits
browning in the stove,
and the clang of the old brass bell
beside her grandma's kitchen door,
calling workers to
the loamy fields.

With no regret she chose
that brighter morn
too vivid to deny.

TO MY LOST GRANDFATHER

I never knew your eyes, your touch, your smell.
In my childhood no one spoke your name.
"Things best not talked about,"
my grandmother said when I asked.
I have but fragments of your sundered lives—
a letter, a poem, a divorce decree,
no other proof of your existence,
except my father's birth.
I cannot tell my children
the dates carved upon your tomb.

One old aunt claimed you wrote
letters to my grandmother
that her brother intercepted.
"You're gone. Now stay gone,"
he wrote, returning them all.
All but the one she kept hidden
in her trunk, a holy relic
till the day she died.
It said you loved her and your son
but had to go—
go where?
and why?

What hidden secrets
were worth a toddler's smile,
a woman's soft thighs
and tender heart,
an empty branch?

Your voice leaves no echo.
No tatter of memory
helps shape the face
I so long to know.

I can send you
only greetings
from a stranger,
grandfather,
wherever
your bones may lie.

GRANDMOTHER AT PRAYER

The family kneels in lamplight,
as she recites the evening prayers.
Ghosts from an unsaid past
hover in shadowed corners
of the room. I see them there.
I do not know their names.

Beside her on the cold
wood floor is the gentle man,
her husband now,
who loves her, inarticulate,
but fails to touch
the deep core reserved
for the man who went away.

Her voice rises above the gloom,
to tell God of their griefs,
their needs, their hopes of Heaven.
She praises His name
in toneless ritual.
"Thy will be done."

She knows His will,
but it is not her own.
She bit down on her lot in life,
testing its metal, believing it to be
without the value of that
unalloyed gold she thinks she's lost
resigning herself to lesser coin
that leaves a bitter taste.

She rarely smiles.
Her words to that good man,

who helped to raise her sons
are only "Bring in some wood,"
and "Get the eggs,"
and "Did you turn off all the lamps?"
Never once have I seen her touch his hand
or meet his eyes with tenderness.
She never speaks of the other—
the one no longer there.
Her ardent prayers,
alleged conversations with God,
are the only words
she sends beyond the gloom,
beyond this life of arid soil,
to him whose face I never knew
and she has half forgot.

The dimmed oil lamp
casts silhouettes against the wall,
as she sends forth her messages
of wild honey and of gall
into the chill of night,
to her absent god—
the unforgiven man
she once loved.

Prayers at an end, she rises
and bids good night to all.
Her husband follows
her silent tread.
Together, they enter
the darkness of their room,
but when she shuts the door,
she shuts herself alone inside.

PAPA GAILEY

He used to wait to watch the trains go by,
sitting on the front porch of the house
dreaming of distant lands he used to know
when he was in the navy years ago.

At four each afternoon the whistle blew.
Standing by then, he'd raise his wrinkled hand,
for he would hear it coming down the track.
The engineers waved back; they knew him well,

that white-haired man who lived across the road
from where the tracks ran silver through the fields.
He'd be there every day, the trainmen knew,
faithful at his watch as they passed through.

Then one day he was gone. The word spread fast,
"Old Gailey passed," they heard along the line.
As years went by his absence was still felt
The empty porch fell into disrepair,

and strangers came to occupy the place.
But engineers still blew their whistles there
as they passed by the graveyard where he lay
beside the track just down the road a way.

I'd like to think he still awaits the train
to raise his ghostly hand as it goes by.
Though he never got away or rode the cars,
his spirit sailed those engines to the sky.

RETURN TO BUCKHEAD

At first I almost wish I hadn't come.
The house, swept clean of all I knew,
seems wrong—like a place I've never been before.

Weeds and grass now grow in that broom-swept yard,
where spreading roots of ancient trees once sheltered
tea parties, with paper dolls and cracked china plates.
The trees are gone—victim to a lightning strike, I'm told.

But once inside, memory banishes Pergo floors, big-screen TV,
central heat and air. Old walls rise up again,
permeated with familiar smells of cedar-stored linens,
sugary jam, and the Franklin stove still burning
in the room where the old couple sleep and pass their days.

There she sits, bent away from the scrollwork
of carved oak, frowning over her King James text,
in the chair that rocked five generations of our family,
too short for modern legs, but cut to her frail frame.

In the kitchen the iron cook stove hides neat piles
of splintered logs, brought from the woodpile by Patsy,
who fetched the sticks, cut small to fit her canine jaws.

When company comes, the woman thinks nothing
of frying a pullet for breakfast, serving it with hot biscuits,
butter she churned herself, and fig preserves
made from lush fruit, yielding up its soft, pink flesh,
growing on large-leafed limbs outside the window.

The old man makes the biscuits and keeps them
in the stove warmer until it's time to eat.
He'd been a galley chef on the *Mercury* in World War I.
"Best biscuits I ever ate," my mother says every single time.

Outside the kitchen door on the back porch ledge,
morning glory vines shade the water bucket,
a white enameled dipper hanging from a nail, ready
to serve it up, nectar-sweet as corn straight from the field.

The rusting pulley of the well creaks at water's weight.
Beyond looms the unpainted barn where the old man
keeps his mule and stores his tools, his plow,
the hoes and rakes that keep the furrows clear.

Well-worn ruts of road stretch once more beyond the barn,
past the wooden outhouse to skirt the cotton field,
leading toward the big ditch, not yet filled with kudzu,
where I used to find abundant arrowheads.

It all returns in softened colors but sharp clear lines.
I will not come again, I think, not trusting memory twice.
I drive away—the western sky filling with light
as the east grows dim, preparing to trim the night with stars.

III. POEMS OF THE ARTS

ON COMING UPON THE GRAVE OF ANDREW LYTLE AT THE SEWANEE WRITERS CONFERENCE

There you lie —
beneath the crusty soil of dry late-summer days
and curvature of vines — name-carved in granite.
How strange that I should find you here
after decades of indifference, just when
I've laid aside those unproductive days.

A gray squirrel brattles through deposits
of amber leaves
as I sift dry layers of years
and wonder that I've come upon you now,
in the midst of this quiet walk
on my own stalk of resurgence —
as though I've circled back to where I left off,
poised to start again.

Beside you lies your wife, dying when,
teacher, student, we first met.
I didn't know and, ensnared as I still was
in the unformed ways of youth,
could not understand how love and grief
absorb one's life away from paltry things
like young-novice literary skills.

But then I had to live your days,
when all I cared about went slipping
through these fingers that could not hold it back,
when I watched my own beloved slip away
and learned the lesson of incapacitating loss.

It's no doubt fitting that I stumble upon you
here—where recognition and regret clatter
through the branches above these standing stones
to mark my graveyard of lost fertile days.

STARRY NIGHT

in tribute to William Carlos Williams

In Van Gogh's great painting *Starry Night,*
the heavens swirl in vortices of stars
and blazing crescent moon's unfurling light,
like vapor curling through the dark-blue void,
slashed by the flame-shaped black of twisted tree,
while in the quiet village down below
a steeple rises upward toward the sky
where one star, pearl-brighter than the rest,
hovers over the town and seems to lure
the wise madman locked up in Saint-Rémy,
whose whirling mind has conjured up the scene
in Van Gogh's great painting *Starry Night.*

THE CRAFT AND SULLEN ART

"The lif so short, the craft so long to lerne."
Chaucer, *Parliament of Fowls*

Only a fool becomes a poet now.
This art and craft are valueless to most,
when only lucre and vapid fame allow
for recognition by the *Morning Post*.
But I'm a fool and always have been so,
trying things wise people should reject
and rushing in where I should never go.
It's not my only flaw, though I suspect
it's my nature to take the path less sure
that leads me on to sites I can't foresee,
following ways that seem the most obscure
to places I was somehow meant to be.

But when I took this path, I didn't know
it was a craft I never could forego.

WATER DREAMS

I dreamed
cascades of poems
last night
waterfalls of words
pouring over rocks
disturbing sleep
but now
they've vanished
dry as dawn
as I stare
at blank paper
pen in hand
my mind
as arid
as the flat
blue lines
that stretch
across
the page
and tumble
from the edge

Last night
droplets of words
formed torrents
that flowed
wildly coherent
into verse
carving out riverbeds
that drought
of day has all
but turned to dust.

POEM

Read
read me
read me on
to the end
of the printed page
against the time
when I will be reduced
to electronic impulses
that lack the smell of ink
and the smooth texture
of fibers interlocked,
where there is no place
for scribbled notes
and I am stored in
some hard pantechnicon
of bits and bytes

She made me into words
so I would last
and be substantial
well beyond this day
but when I am as deletable
as a cameo carved in soap
will I still survive
such hazards
as malevolent viruses
intended obsolescence
downed power lines
and dead batteries
or even simple things
like being dropped into bath water
or thrown in anger across a room?

Or must I
like this paper bed
on which I lie
await my own extinction?

SOLITARY HARPIST AT THE SEWANEE MUSIC FESTIVAL

Beneath an archway of the colonnade
a pierced-tongue girl in tattered jeans
strokes taut strings on a pedal harp
and teases out sweet moans of harmony.

From the window of my room I watch,
eavesdropping on this tryst of hands and harp.
Six hundred years fade in a finished chord,
and I can see her dressed in a silken gown,

blue and flowing, embroidered at the neck.
It hides her ankles and her silver shoes.
Behind her, large oak double doors lead
to the great hall where her lover waits

to feed her sugared grapes and cup his hand
to catch the seeds her blemished tongue expels.

CONCOURS POÉTIQUE

They like the literary poems,
shot through with allusive names
that carry baggage of their own —
Belaqua, Demeter, Laudine.
It's better if they're laced
with visions of the natural world,
the soaring kestrel and milkweed pods.
And they like them long,
divided into numbered sections,
dense, dull, obscure,
accessible only to the lettered few.

But I don't give a damn.
My pain's too great, my loss too deep
to rarify into some Orphic quest.
The prize will go to someone else.
But spilled out on this crumpled page
are my raw bones, my skinless flesh
trying to heal, my gaping mouth
trying to find the words
to speak my grief.

Must all be writ in musty retrospect?
Can no fresh blood be spilled upon the page?

Let them work their will.
I do not write for them.
I write for you,
my sister, my brother,
walking wounded of this earth
who stand beside me
in your own anguish
and can understand.

They are the judges.
Let them stand apart
and judge.

IV. ANIMAL AND NATURE POEMS

LAYOVER IN CINCINNATI

A gray-breasted sparrow,
black against clerestory windows
of the C concourse waiting area,
flaps frenzied wings against the glass.
I hear her chirps above
the din of gate announcements,
passenger complaints, chatter
of monitors blaring Fox News.
She disappears from time to time,
then returns, more urgent than before.

I watch her futile fluttering
for half an hour
until my flight is called.
Handing my boarding pass
to the attendant, I look back.
Still she flails against the glass,
seeking open air.
I wonder if she'll be there
next time I fly though —
bones upon the window ledge.

RETURN FROM RUSSIA

My yard is parched from summer drought.
It has collected early falling leaves
and drunk nothing in my absence
but fiercely rationed dew.
Now every blade of grass has died.
Thoughtless of growing things left behind,
I reveled instead in onion domes
and icons and a cappella choirs
and returned to this well-deserved ruin.

In past years, it might have found redemption
in afternoon storms and fierce watery winds,
but this year no rain, no sound but dry thunder,
the roar of truck tires on hot tarmac,
and the desiccated screeches
of dog-day cicadas, here to witness
the browning blades of my once-green lawn
and sing their final mournful dirge
as dry grass crumbles into arid soil.

ENTR'ACTE

Winter sun
breaks through
dry oak leaves
to spotlight
the ballet of birds
feasting as they dance.
Three, now four,
chickadees and titmice
peck at the seeds.
The feeder rocks
in rhythm
as they prance
and pause
and perch
along its wires,
hammering out
the cadence
with their beaks
to penetrate
the seeded block.

A gray cat slouches
in slow rhythm
across the yard.
The feeder empties,
sways and stills,
a vacant stage
still gleaming
in the winter sun.

SUNDAY MORNING IN KEY WEST

The rooster
plants himself
in the middle

of Duval Street
and raises
his head

to crow at
oncoming
traffic

before strutting
slowly
to the curb.

METAMORPHOSIS

They used to call me Robespierre.
I pecked and pinched
those vicious children
who poked their fingers
in my cage and tried
to make me eat dead flies
and failed to bring me water.
They thought me ill-tempered,
for I squawked and bit
as often as I could.

So they gave me away
to their grandmother,
who cooed at me
in the mornings and warbled
words from long ago.
She fed me birdseed
and bits of buttered toast
from off her plate.

She took me on her finger
from my cage, let me ride
on her soft, wrinkled shoulder
and gave me water to drink
from her cupped hand.
She changed my name
to Sweetpea, and so I sang
her welcome in the mornings
and chirped when she arose,
glad to see me every day.

SPRING DAY IN SEATTLE

Drops of blue seep through
the Douglas firs,
looming dark against
the May-end sky,
darker against
the tender green of
bloomed-out apple limbs.
Old trees hang
their branches low,
while those just
springing green
lift leafy twig-arms
toward the sun
and whisper warm
against my back.
An Anna's hummingbird
at arm's length
competes with bees
for nectar
from the drooping stars
of columbine
that sway so gently
to the wind's baton.

REVISIT

The hummingbird
is there again
this morning,
sipping as always
from the flowery cup.
Her brevity
at the nectary,
her pauses in mid-air
as she looks toward
the glass door
where I stand,
coffee in hand,
make me wonder
whether she really
came to fill her crop,
or did she come
from curiosity,
wondering *who
is the woman
standing there,
watching me
every day?*
With one last glance,
one more taste,
she darts away.
I trust she'll come
tomorrow
for our breakfast
rendezvous.

WINTER FRAGMENT

a dusting of snow on the roadway
like flour sifted on the castle floor
to catch a lover's footprints
in the night

SPRING FRAGMENT

the first robin's egg of spring
the brave promise
of its fragile blue shell
no more protection
than the single thorn
of a simple rose
growing alone
on a far-off
asteroid.

DAY OF THE EMPRESS

She is always first to rise,
walking on my sleeping face
to proclaim the day begun.
On the sunniest portion
of the antique Gansu rug
she takes her morning naps
until I settle down to read,
when she prefers her comfort
in the center of my open book
and demands to be stroked.

She rewards my efforts
with rumbling gratitude
or scratchy licks of tongue.
For exercise, a midday stroll
up and down piano keys,
followed by an afternoon doze
on the western windowsill.
Then, coiling herself around my legs,
she informs me it's time to serve
dinner on her flowered china plate.

ECLIPSE ON MOUNT WASHINGTON ON A CLOUDY NIGHT

The moon is twice eclipsed
and gives no light,
only fluorescent stars,
reflected at our feet,
bleed pastel colors
where three rivers join,
like running chalk
from sidewalk art
in an unexpected rain.

UNCLE ED'S HOUND DOG

As the afternoon wanes
he listens on the front porch
as dozens of cars roll by,

head resting on his paws,
eyes closed but one ear cocked.
When the whirring motor

he knows so well
tops the roadway's rise,
his tail begins to thump

against the painted boards.
He raises his head and lumbers up
to amble down the wooden steps.

Tail wagging welcome,
he waits, ready in the gravel drive,
to greet his master home.

SUMMER DAYS HAVE NO BONES

Summer days have no bones
and I move or am still
wrist-free of time
to read the hours
in sun and shadow.

Dew sparkles on the grass
as I have strawberries
and ice cream for breakfast
or sit in my garden
with my absent poet friend,
to catch a scent of honeysuckle
on a random breeze.
When a cloud shadows my world
I sometimes nap.

The moment lingers,
deliciously enigmatic,
until daylilies close
and the sky blinks periwinkle,
until children yawn
and fireflies beacon the garden.

Summer days are leftover puddles
for frogs and toes
or tiny paper boats
happily going nowhere.

SUBDIVISION RISING

Last July
it was a living field
of Queen Anne's Lace,
white morning glories,
purple thistles,
red trumpet creepers
climbing wild privet
at its edge.
One oak tree
stood sentinel
at its center —
a child's garden
a firefly arena,
a rabbit haunt.

This July
the field is rubble
dried clumps of dirt,
wildflowers plowed under,
replaced by pipes and wires
and roads, where
skeletons of houses,
all much alike,
rise up around
the single oak.

Oakfield they call it,
having lost all else
to bear its name.

V. POEMS OF LOVE AND LOSS

VALENTINE

This paper begs for pressure from a pen.
It longs to be inscribed with secret thoughts,
memories, confessions of a wayward heart,
to witness our being like a seal in hot wax.

The pen will leave behind indelible marks
for there is no eraser, no undo key,
no way to unsay what we commit
to writing on this old-fashioned paper heart.

But if we choose to make a valentine,
what does it matter if words should prove
but transient truth and leave false record
for the attic trunk? It's far better

to disturb the dust and set ephemera
upon the page than leave no trace at all.

PHOTO FOR A SECOND MARRIAGE

There we stand
in perpetual embrace,
your lips parted in an unformed phrase,
expression sweetly vulnerable.
My eyes smile,
gazing toward late-summer's
canopy of maple leaves.
Our rings gleam new gold.
In that still moment
between past and future,
we are two birds poised for flight
through faintly fall-tinged leaves,
not yet mindful of the winter snow.

CONTRACEPTIVE

Your body magnetized to mine
the ancient storied ritual
told against the days and nights

when blackbirds called
or seagulls screeched
we made love to ward off death

and bring the rain
you splashed into me
swimmers against the current

upstream like salmon
for the same purpose
had we not blocked the way

but dam we did and now
I have no daughter
but regret

VIRIDITAS

Had I been your sister
I would have held you
and kissed you
and rocked your cradle.
I would have protected you
from cats and drafts
and held your hand
when we crossed the street together.
I would have shown you
violets and buttercups
and caterpillars and acorns
and awakened you to the world.

Now it is you who awaken me
to stars and worlds of wonder,
implications,
intimations,
imbrications
never dreamed,
to poets and crystal planets
and the greening power of love.

WITHOUT GOODBYE

We had no time
to say goodbye.
When I left you
the night before,
I kissed
your moist forehead.
You tried
to squeeze my hand,
whispering
with all the strength
you could muster,
"I love you."
I whispered back
and held you

o too briefly

then fled,
weeping
in the winter cold
outside,
to the haven
of our home.

I had not known
that night would be
our last goodbye,
our only one.
and yet I must have known
in some subliminal way,
for when the nurse's call
came in the early dawn,
I knew the message

before the words were said.
Awakened earlier
by a phantom ring,
I had already
tasted the bitter hemlock
of fear
and void
and endless night.

THE GARDEN

Our garden is empty now
of all but lilies and mock orange,
of all but hyacinths and primrose,
Saint Francis stands alone among the liriope
his arms open to receive the birds.

Our garden is empty now,
of all but robins and gray squirrels,
of all but dragonflies and hummingbirds,
an occasional swallowtail,
and a once-in-a-while grosbeak.

If only you were a perennial,
I could be like Ceres
and let you go for just the winter.
But to do without you in the spring
is more than even God should ask.

HAIKU

You are with me still
in the garden of my mind
planting the hostas.

ANNIVERSARY: FEBRUARY 8, 2011

Twenty years today I closed your eyes
and held your hand till your skin
grew cold beneath my touch.
Dust moats floated in the winter light
on empty hospital air.
But still I felt your presence there —
until the children talked me home.

Later, your body lay abandoned,
dressed in your best suit,
artificial color added to your face.
I placed a winter flower from our garden
in the hand of your empty remains
and had the coffin closed.

But part of you stayed with me still.
In the spring you whispered love
in an unplanted row of red salvia
blooming along the veranda edge,
and then, in our island home,
I found your token — a red plastic heart
etched with the final words
you spoke to me.

In time, you quietly slipped away,
leaving this world
a dim and foreign land.
Sometimes I let myself forget
you are gone,
only to be surprised again by grief —
the price of love — still lurking
in the shadows of the day.

THE GIFT

If words can be my only gift to you,
then let them float like feathers,
not weigh you down like promises.

Let them shine on moonlit shores,
where lovers' footprints
vanish with the tide.

Let them delight like rainbows
that evanesce, leaving
only brightness in their wake.

Let them enhance your dreams,
then fade to leave you free
in the daylight of your life.

Let them settle softly in your heart,
like caresses from a vision
or the brush of an angel's wing

and echo there like whispers,
carried on the wind of things
that briefly were.

LOVE

Why do you come again
like a deceitful crocus,
awakening my garden
with fragrance
and life-hopes
and wearisome once-agains?

BILLETS DOUX

You spoke of immortal diamonds,
but your love was air and milkweed,
blown here and there, nestled among thorns,
choked by vines, dried by drought.
People moved about us unaware
as if we were dry sticks of wood
waiting to be burned. Perhaps we were.
At least I've burned those empty words,
emptier than those you sometimes read
to people gathered in half-empty halls,
eager for the masticated meaning
you spit out with such authority.

Those words too may prove
in time no more than air and milkweed,
though they still float in unfilled halls
where someone, someday,
may collect their tenuous fibers,
separate them from the dust,
and weave them into an unread volume
to lie, forgotten, as your love,
on musty shelves.

WEEKEND ON THE MOUNTAIN

We sat on the edge of the world.
The dappled sky stretched over us
its blue-grey canopy.
My tears fell like rain into the valley
which dropped below, half lost in primal mist.
You held me as I wept out all my grief.
You held me back from the precipice
into which I could have fallen
without your strong arms.
Saturday on the mountain.

Reverberating, rising song,
nourished by Eucharist
and stained-glass sunshine.
No mists today.
We find the cool depths of the forest
below the great stone bridge
where we stand solid, side by side,
looking down on the brighter earth below.
No fear of falling now.
Sunday on the mountain.

And in the years to come,
many or few as they shall be,
I will remember these days
and lift up my eyes
to see once more the mountain
where you gave me strength.

FIRST LOVE

Cotton candy, fresh sawdust,
the caramel of Crackerjacks,
red and yellow spotlights
flashing ring to ring
kaleidoscope before his eyes.
At their center a slender girl,
young, lithe, supple
as a willow branch,
soars on a trapeze
high over the middle ring.
Her beauty cracks his heart.

Descended, she smiles, waves,
slips through a fissure in the tent.
Cyclists wheel in to fill her empty spot.
The boy half-watches and waits
for the girl to reappear,
as riders do headstands
on whirling wheels,
clowns and tigers steal the show,
until they too follow her
through the slash of tent
and lights fade—a gritty dawn.

Now cotton candy, clowns
tigers, tent, and girl are gone.
All morning and all afternoon
the boy practices in the driveway
his own bicycle tricks,
stretching his body
toward the unknown,
the less understood,
thinking to join the circus
when it next comes through town.

LOVE AFTER PRIME

He is hers on Thursday afternoons.
They hide their love, not wanting
to seem foolish in a world where
only youth and unblemished beauty
are deemed worthy of such fierce
and turbulent passion.

Their bodies are no longer fresh
and scarless, but reshaped
by gravity, loss, unnumbered hours
behind a desk or before an easel.
It is too late, they know,
to make a life together.

He is mired in loveless marriage,
with children and grandchildren
to consider. She is widowed and devout.
They are too old and respected to cause
such scandal. Yet they love in secret
as they have never loved before.

One incomplete
without the other.

When they embrace,
naked as young lovers do,
they see with aging eyes
soft wrinkled flesh still firm and sweet
with the taste of apples,
the smell of hyacinths.

And when he dies—a death so sudden—
the town turns out in droves
to mourn his loss. She does not
attend the funeral, but sends a card
of condolence to his unloved wife,
wraps herself in a blanket,

and weeps alone.

VI. POEMS FOR THE MEDIEVAL SOUL

TAPESTRY

This tapestry takes shape—
its woof and warp
from multivocal threads
of variegated shades,
from filaments of life
or shreds of ancient books,
or fibers from the tatters
of a dream.

Bright patterns
surface unexpectedly,
shot from this shuttle
of a pen, woven
on this paper loom,
contexture crafted
giving form to things
too often left unsaid
in the quotidian world
of bills and taxes

where colors fade to gray
and knots untie.

SONNET À MON BEL AMI

I am bound to you in holy ways,
in mystic ways that lie beyond this world.
Our hands have surely touched before this life,
and we have lain in one another's arms.

Beneath the ash tree on the riverbank
where swam the snowy swans of Caerleon,
we've spread our blanket many times before
and shared these kisses from the breath of God.

As long as there is time and space and life,
our souls will meet in greening fields like these.
So take this heart I give you once again.
Stretch out your hand to meet me, o my love,

that I may feel its healing grace once more
and kiss the fingertips these times have touched.

HELOISE AND ABELARD SEQUENCE

I. HELOISE TO ABELARD

Oh, that you were my brother
who sucked at the breasts of my mother,
how simple would be our lot
and what anguish we'd be spared.

Now set me as a seal upon your heart.
Indelible and silent,
let me stay.
I ask no more.

Just love me all my life,
and at my death,
come stand beside my grave
and grieve,
my brother,
my lover.

II. TOMB OF HELOISE AND ABELARD

Beneath this portico
lie two marble effigies
side by side.
They do not touch.
Their hands rise up in prayer
above their marble breasts,
his face stern, head tonsured,
an abbot's calm façade.
Beside him sleeps his wife,
her hair concealed
beneath an abbess's wimple,
both properly portrayed
in guise of willing supplication.

A sudden burst of sun
breaks through the clouds
to strike two smaller
swirling portraits in bas-relief,
high on the angled pediments,
capturing the pair as they were
before their cloistered lives.

Her right bosom peeks above
the draping cloth; open eyes
look straight ahead.
Her head is bare, her hair,
like his, full and flowing.
His strong chin is squared,
mouth full and sensual,
as it was when he sang her praise
in bawdy Paris taverns
and kissed her parted lips.

Unlike the *gisants* below,
passive, obedient, still,
shadowed in the portico,
the bright figures above
resist their circles, lean forward
to face the elements head-on.
Undaunted by rain or sun,
they strain against all circumscription
to defy the marble's limitation —
portraits of the brazen pair
before sharp retribution.

III. PÈRE LACHAISE

I stand in reverence
beside the silent tomb
of Abelard and Heloise,
littered with dying blossoms
left by admirers, hearts
perhaps constricted
by the savage pathos
of their story.

Two lovers hand-in-hand
stroll down the cemetery path.
She brings a yellow rose.
They come to join me
in my reverie, I presuppose.
But they pass me by
without a glance, seeking the one
to whom they've come to pay respect.
I hear their American accents
as they stop to ask a caretaker
farther along the walk,
*"Où se trouve la tombe
de Jim Morrison?"*

He's heard the question
many times before
and points them on their way.
What could they know
of Heloise and Abelard?
And why would they want
to know it? Sufficient are
the sorrows of our day.

LAÜSTIC°
(in tribute to a lai of Marie de France)

I sent him the dead bird,
wrapped in white samite,
embroidered to tell
the tale of love's demise.
Whether he will understand
or not, who can say?
He was content
to share the nightbird's song,
the bodiless erotic
words from darkened windows.
But he never sent for me.

Awakened by the nightingale,
the fleshy man rose from
our empty bed and seized
the tiny bird in jealous rage.
He wrung its neck and spattered
its blood on the bosom
of my gown.
A hostile bird he called it
and served it up for dinner
on shiny plates.
I did not eat.

° *Laüstic* is the Breton word for nightingale. *Samite* is an elegant and heavy silk fabric woven with a gold or silver thread, used in the Middle Ages in particularly regal and sacramental contexts.

ELEANOR

She floats into the hall,
bedecked in golden silk,
a diaphanous cloud
on a twisted tree.
Eustace is dead,
choked on a plate of eels
that ended his hunger
for the throne.

They say she once
lay on a purple couch,
opened her thighs
and sealed the fate
of a fraught crusade.
But she is no fool,
and in the end
she will be queen again.

BURGUNDIAN MIRROR, 15ᵗʰ CENTURY

Molded in a perpetual state
the man offers a flower
to a lady not his wife,
though she wears a matching
blossom at her waist.
His stance is arrogant.
Her hand is raised —
in a gesture of surprise?
an effort to refuse?
or is she reaching
out to take it?
She floats
above the ground,
where his feet
are firmly planted.
For six hundred years
they have stood thus,
not touched, nor smiled,
this waiting lover
and his ivory lady.

THE POSTULATE
**(STUDENT FIELD TRIP TO THE
CONVENT OF THE SACRED HEART)**

Little sister, pretty as a spring lilac,
without a veil, yet cloistered all the same,
your choice is mystery to those
whose lives are fixed on rap and rock
and weekends soothed by boys and beer.

Your tranquility, so at odds
with their frenetic quest,
evokes their nervous laughter.
They cannot understand
your blossoming in this peaceful glen.

Where they see withered stalks,
and hear but empty silence,
you see a world evergreen,
melodious with birdsong and
unity in the vespers voice.

You wave goodbye as they leave
in the autumn afternoon
to ride in silence back to their world
of shopping malls and busy bars,
the noisy cadence of their lives.

CHEVREFOIL*

You thrust it,
half-crushed,
into my hand,
but it still gave off
a heady scent
as we met again
on that flagstone terrace
outside of Belfast.
For one still
twilight moment
we touched
each other's hands
and let the vine
wrap us round
once more.

Language is insufficient,
but we both understand
and misunderstand
non-language just as well,
as we learned
that dying afternoon,
when honeysuckle
broke through walls
as no words could
and freed us
from the prisons
of ourselves.

---

* *Chevrefoil* is the Old French word for honeysuckle. It is also the title of a *lai* about Tristan and Iseut, written by Marie de France.

LYRIC

Afterwards,

when your hand grows heavy
on my breast and sleep is good,

when the thunder is still
and your back is smooth
and moist and gently heaving.

when the stars are clear
and the night's breath sweet brushed
with cricket songs,

you dream of bright ladies
riding unicorns in the dew
and singing wistful melodies.

THE THREAD BOX

*FOUND IN THE GRAVE OF AN ANGLO-SAXON
WOMAN AT NORTH LEIGH, OXFORDSHIRE*

It hung suspended from a leather sash
tied about her waist and dangled
      at her side on metal links—a flash
      of silver when she walked that jangled
          like tiny ill-toned bells.
Its perforations gave off a musty smell
of crushed herbs wrapped in pungent pelt,
of slow-healing scars of flesh and soul—
redolent of pain or joy still deeply felt.

Inside are fibers, unraveled from a garment
or plucked from regal cloth still in the weaving
      for a wedding, perhaps, or even rent
      on some occasion for her grieving,
          torn from a loved one's shroud.
All the fragments she kept within were endowed
with sweet memory or loss that pierced her heart,
with suffering borne in private by the bearer,
but from others' knowledge always set apart.

Now here it lies on this museum shelf
exposed to the view of gawking passers-by—
      a relic—remnants of her inner self.
      Tourists gape with calloused eyes
          at her once sacred past,
at this token she deemed worthy to hold fast
and bear her secrets—so precious they've
been borne from life to immortality
and laid beside her in her barrow grave.

ACKNOWLEDGMENTS

The poems listed below have been previously published, some in slightly different forms. Thanks to the editors of the books and journals where they first appeared.

"Beach Walk," *Basilica Review*
"First Love," *Maypop Magazine*
"North End Beach," *Jekyll Island: The Nearest Faraway Place*
"On Coming Upon the Grave of Andrew Lytle," *Time and Tradition: A Poetry Anthology*
"Paper Fish," *Time and Tradition*
"Reconciliation," *Time and Tradition*
"Solitary Harpist," *Time and Tradition*
"Subdivision Rising," *Time and Tradition*
"The Mourner," *Time and Tradition*
"To the Islands in December," *Basilica Review*
"Viriditas," *Time and Tradition*

I also thank the following people for their comments, suggestions, and encouragement at various stages in the writing and publishing of these poems: Michelle Adkerson, Billy Collins, Kay Day, Michael Dumanis, Sara Dunne, Kerri French, Philip Mathis, Margaret Ordoubadian, Jennie Grace Ragland, the late Mark Strand, Maggi Britton Vaughn, Marjory Wentworth, and the members of the Murfreesboro Writers Group.

www.ingramcontent.com/pod-product-compliance
Lightning Source LLC
Chambersburg PA
CBHW071720040426
42446CB00011B/2149